A
Trail
Of
Tears

Bible Study For Lent

Robert C. Bankhead

CSS Publishing Company, Inc., Lima, Ohio

A TRAIL OF TEARS

Copyright © 2001 by
CSS Publishing Company, Inc.
Lima, Ohio

Scripture quotations marked (NRSV) are from the *New Revised Standard Version of the Bible*, copyright 1989 by the Division of Christian Education of the National Council of the Churches of Christ in the USA. Used by permission.

For more information about CSS Publishing Company resources, visit our website at www.csspub.com.

ISBN 0-7880-1857-4   PRINTED IN U.S.A.

Dedicated to
The Session and Members
Carolina Beach Presbyterian Church

The Gospels As Passion Narratives

A series of seven Bible studies for Lent, tracing the life of Jesus from the retreat with the disciples to Caesarea Philippi through the crucifixion, death, and burial. The study focuses on the three Synoptic Gospels. It is appropriate for use in any of the three years of the Lectionary Calendar.

A Word To The Bible Study Group Leader

Current scholarship focuses attention on the Gospels as separate, individual stories of the life of Jesus, each written with a theological inclination for a different community of early church believers. The gospel task is to discern what the community was like for which Matthew, or Mark, or Luke, or John wrote the Gospel. Earlier attempts to forge a harmony of the life of Jesus from the several Gospels are no longer the focal point of Gospel studies.

Proposing a Bible Study of the Gospels as Expanded Passion Narratives, using all three synoptic Gospels, is not intended to produce a harmony of the gospel. Quite to the contrary, it affirms the quest to discern the nature and character of the early church community for which each Gospel was written. It is crucial in understanding each Gospel to ask what the community reading this Gospel was like. Why did the Gospel writer choose to write as he did? Why did he select certain details to include and choose to omit other facts? What can we learn about the community of faith by the form of the canonical Gospel as it has been passed down to us?

There is, however, a common element in the character of the Gospels. All have a nucleus of reporting the Passion, which was the kernel of faith from which the story of Jesus evolved. Each writer organized and developed the story in different ways. From this varied development we learn about the community to which the Gospel was written.

As a Bible study leader of a group, you may wish to direct some discussion during class periods to questions of why and how the gospel was different. Try to discover the nature and character of the community for which each Gospel was written.

Lesson 1

Three Predictions Of The Passion

Texts: Mark 8:31;   9:31;   10:32-34
          Matthew 16:21;   17:22-23;   20:17-19
          Luke 9:22;   9:44;   18:31-33

Themes: Framework and Structure of the Passion Narrative
          The Character of the Gospels

The Character Of The Gospels

The Synoptic Gospels have been characterized as expanded Passion Narratives. It is thought that the earliest stories of the life of Jesus were oral repetitions focused on his death and resurrection. Short accounts of Jesus' suffering and death were most likely gathered in collections and handed down by word of mouth, until they were written and incorporated into the emerging Gospels.

The church's earliest preaching was shaped by the two salvation events of crucifixion and resurrection. Peter set the pattern in his first sermon on the day of Pentecost, "This man (Jesus of Nazareth) ... you crucified and killed ... But God raised him up" (Acts 2:23-24; and cf. Acts 2:32, 36). Compare this text with other early preaching in Acts 3:14-15; 4:10; 5:30-31; and 10:39-40.

The first creed of the church, the Corinthian formula, 1 Corinthians 15:3-5, confessed faith in the saving events.

*Christ died for our sins in accordance with the
    Scriptures;
He was buried;
He was raised on the third day in accordance with the
    Scriptures;
He appeared to Cephas, then to the Twelve.*

From this confessional form the stories of Jesus developed in reverse, moving back from the death-resurrection to Jesus' final visit to Jerusalem, where he was arrested, accused of blasphemy and sedition by the Jewish authorities, tried and sentenced to death by the Roman governor, and crucified. The Passion Narrative became the core of early Christian Theology, defining the sacrifice of Jesus Christ as Savior, dying for the redemption of all who believed in him. The apostles' preaching emphasized the theme of salvation through Jesus' Passion-Crucifixion-Resurrection. "There is salvation in no one else, for there is no other name ... by which we must be saved" (Acts 4:12), and "God exalted him at God's right hand as Leader and Savior that he might give repentance to Israel and forgiveness of sins" (Acts 5:31).

The expansion of the Gospels backwards continued with additions of other stories of Jesus' public ministry, eventually including in Matthew and Luke narratives of his birth. The church was struggling to define for its own understanding and faith just who this Jesus, born in Bethlehem, reared in Nazareth, and crucified in Jerusalem, really was.

The Gospels thus developed as theologically oriented biographies of his life. Not intended to be historical accounts, with the details expected of a carefully researched biography, they were focused to define the person and work of the Christ, sent by God for the salvation of the world. Each writer selected and included details to depict Jesus as he felt critical for the community of faith for which he was writing.

The shape of the Gospel as an expanded Passion Narrative was determined by Jesus' prediction of his impending death, dividing his life and ministry into two periods: his public ministry and his passion and death. The pattern is clearly discernible in the Gospel of Mark, generally recognized as the first Gospel to be gathered, collated, and written. Over half of Mark (8:31—15:47) describes the final journey to Jerusalem, his last week in the holy city, and his death and burial. Almost one-third is devoted to the final week of his life, and almost one-fifth relates the final 48 hours. The account of the resurrection is short in Mark (16:1-8), including only eight verses in the original form, leaving the fact of

10

the resurrection unclear and confusing, with the disciples hiding in fear, not knowing what to do. In Matthew and Luke the resurrection increased in significance as narratives of the appearances of the risen Lord to more believers were added.

Recurrent Themes

The Passion Narrative in the Gospels is composed around three repeated themes:
1) Jesus' Predictions of His Death
2) Increasing Isolation and Growing Conflict
3) A Travel Narrative of His Journey to Jerusalem.

Matthew introduces all three themes in his account of Jesus' first prediction of the Passion, "Jesus began to show his disciples that he must go to Jerusalem and undergo great suffering at the hands of the elders and chief priests and scribes, and be killed, and on the third day be raised" (Matthew 16:21). All three are found in each of the synoptic Gospels, but different themes are emphasized in the different Gospels. Mark's narrative is structured by the three predictions of Jesus' impending death. Generally accepted as the earliest written Gospel, and recognized as a primary source for Matthew and Luke, Mark is often credited with shaping the Gospel format. It establishes the framework of the developing narrative.

In Matthew and Mark the basic structure traces 1) Jesus' increasing isolation from the disciples as they failed to comprehend his approaching suffering and death, and 2) the growing conflict between Jesus and the Jewish leaders, culminating in his arrest, trial, and crucifixion. Through this section Matthew follows Mark more closely than does Luke, adding material from the "sayings of Jesus" source, i.e. "Q" and from a separate Matthean source.

Luke is quite different. The primary theme of Luke's narrative describes the final journey to Jerusalem, which Mark virtually ignores and Matthew notes only in passing. In Luke the Travel Narrative is characterized by the repeated, relentless declaration that Jesus was driven to the city where he would suffer and die. The theme is introduced in Luke 9:51, shortly after the second prediction of the Passion, "When the days drew near for him to be taken up, he set his face to go to Jerusalem." Nothing deterred Jesus from

11

his journey. The theme culminates in a lament for the city, Luke 19:41-44, as Jesus approached Jerusalem on the day of triumphal entry.

The Scandal Of The Cross

The barbaric execution by crucifixion became scandalous with the death of Jesus on the cross. It was inconceivable that the One recognized as the promised Messiah of God be crucified. His ignominious death was abhorrent. That the eternal Son of God suffer as an ordinary human being was the central scandal of Christianity.

The Gospels in their Passion Narratives dealt with the scandal by interpreting Jesus' death as the fulfillment of God's will. They led believers to understand and accept that the Christ in whom they put their faith willingly and obediently died the cruel, agonizing death of a common, ordinary criminal to save them.

Mark set the tone for this image of Jesus as the crucified Messiah, the suffering Son of God, sent by God to die for the salvation of humankind.

Class Members — Preparation Guide

1. Three Predictions of the Passion

In each of the Synoptic Gospels, Jesus predicts his impending suffering and death three times. The pattern is seen most clearly in Mark, where the verse numbers are almost identical — 8:31; 9:31; and 10:32-34. The pattern is less obvious in Matthew and Luke, but is just as definite.

To trace the pattern, read the parallel accounts in their context.
- First prediction: Read Mark 8:27-33; Matthew 16:13-23; Luke 9:18-22
- Second prediction: Mark 9:30-32; Matthew 17:22-23; Luke 9:43-45
- Third prediction: Mark 10:32-34; Matthew 20:17-19; Luke 18:31-34

As you read each passage, describe how the disciples reacted to Jesus' predictions of the Passion.

2. The Shape of the Gospels

Using the resource sheet (page 14) identify the passages which define the outline of the Gospels.
- The first prediction of the Passion divides the life and ministry of Jesus into two parts. Jesus began the journey to Jerusalem shortly thereafter.
- The Galilean ministry began with Jesus' baptism by John.
- The Triumphal Entry into Jerusalem began Jesus' last week in Jerusalem.
- Jesus' Passion, including the trials, crucifixion, and death, began with his arrest.

The Shape Of The Gospel(s)

Public Ministry — Passion Narrative

First Predictions of the Passion

Jesus' Baptism
by John
    Galilean
    Ministry

Triumphal Entry
into Jerusalem
In Jerusalem
    Passion
    Crucifixion
      Resurrection

Mark

1:9-11		8:31	11:1-11
	In Galilee	Journey	Jerusalem
	1:14—10:1	9:2—10:52	11:1—14:3
			Passion
			14:32—15:20
			Crucifixion
			15:21-47
			Resurrection
			16:1-8

Matthew

	3:13-17	16:21-23	21:1-11
Birth	In Galilee	Journey	Jerusalem
1-2	4:12—19:1	16:21—20:34	21:1—26:35
			Passion
			26:36—27:31
			Crucifixion
			27:32-56
			Resurrection
			28:1-20

Luke

3:21-22		9:22	19:28-40
Birth	In Galilee	Journey	Jerusalem
1-2	4:14—18:30	9:51—19:44	19:41—22:38
			Passion
			22:39—23:25
			Crucifixion
			23:26-56
			Resurrection
			24:1-49

Group Leader — Suggestions For Class Discussion

1. Explore why Mark wrote a precise, focused narrative as he did, devoid of details and teachings of Jesus included in Matthew and Luke. Did he lack the source book of Jesus' sayings (Q), available to Matthew and Luke? Or, as the first Gospel to be written was he trying to form the outline and structure of the story of Jesus so that what the church knew about Jesus would not be lost?

2. Discuss the contributions Mark makes to the study of the life of Jesus. What does Mark offer that the other Gospels do not provide? What would we miss if we did not have Mark?

3. Explore the predictions of the Passion as focal points for the development of the gospel. Discuss the reactions of the disciples to each of the three predictions of Jesus' impending death.

4. Studies of the Gospel of Mark have focused on the Messianic Secret. Jesus commanded the disciples not to tell anyone about him until he had risen from the dead. Perhaps Jesus realized that their continuing failure to understand who he was and their unwillingness to accept his Passion would confuse and hinder their witness to the gospel. They were not yet prepared to assume their role. Only from the other side of the crucifixion-resurrection would they fully comprehend the ministry and mission of Jesus. You may wish to explore the Messianic Secret with the class.

5. Spend some time looking at the shape of the Gospels to see the pattern of the developing story of Jesus' Passion.

Lesson 2

An Account Of Isolation And Conflict

Texts: Matthew 16:1-23;   17:1-9, 22-27;   19:3-15;
          20:17-28;   21:23-46;   22:15-46;
          23:1-39

Themes: Turning Points
          Increasing Isolation from the Disciples
          Growing Conflict between Jesus and the Jewish
          authorities

A Turning Point

In Matthew the turning point in Jesus' life and ministry occurred when he took the disciples to the north for a retreat at Caesarea Philippi (Matthew 16:13-20). On this occasion Jesus asked who they thought him to be. Simon Peter replied for the band, confessing their faith in him as "the Christ, the Son of the Living God." Jesus named Simon "the Rock," and declared "on this Rock" he would build the church.

Until the retreat at Caesarea Philippi, Jesus' ministry had been public, as he traveled among the crowds, preaching the good news of the kingdom of God, teaching the multitudes, and healing the sick, infirm, and lame. Beginning with the retreat he increasingly withdrew from the crowds and directed his teaching and preaching to the band of disciples, training and preparing them for their ministry in establishing the church after his death. Occasions of continuing public ministry on the way to Jerusalem were often followed by private instructions to the disciples, explaining what he had done or taught. Caesarea Philippi was the turning point, from public to private ministry, from an open offering of the gospel to the multitudes to training the disciples to assume their role of leadership in the new people of God. Jesus began the process of turning over his ministry to the disciples, who were to form, shape, and build the church.

Isolation

It is ironic, therefore, that the narratives report a number of occasions in which the disciples failed to understand Jesus and proposed courses of action which were contrary to the divine will. Following each of the predictions of the passion the disciples failed to believe, or refused to accept his impending death. After the first, Peter publicly rebuked Jesus, and Jesus reprimanded Peter (Matthew 16:21-23 // Mark 8:31-33). On the Mount of Transfiguration Peter tried to subvert Jesus' plan by proposing they build three booths, or tabernacles, and remain on the mountain (Matthew 17:1-8 // Mark 9:2-8). The disciples challenged Jesus over blessing children (Matthew 19:13-15 // Mark 10:13-16). After the third prediction of the passion, James and John sought a position of favoritism (Matthew 20:20-28 // Mark 10:35-45), and the other disciples were so angered that Jesus was forced to mediate among them to prevent dissension and fragmentation of their community.

Jesus' isolation from the disciples continued in the Passion Narrative with Judas' conspiracy with the Jewish leaders and the betrayal (Matthew 26:14-16, 20-25 // Mark 14:10-11, 17-21 and Matthew 26:47-50 // Mark 14:43-46). The disciples failed to watch with Jesus as he prayed in the Garden (Matthew 26:36-46 // Mark 14:32-42). Peter denied that he even knew Jesus (Matthew 26:31-35, 69-75 // Mark 14:27-31, 66-72). The isolation culminated in the total abandonment by the band at the time of the arrest (Matthew 26:56 // Mark 14:50). The disciples fled in confusion and fear, and were not even present at the crucifixion. Only the women, who had provided and cared for Jesus since his ministry in Galilee, stood by him at the foot of the cross (Matthew 27:55-56 // Mark 15:40-41).

Conflict

After the retreat to Caesarea Philippi, Jesus' conflict with the Jewish authorities rapidly increased, as they perceived his threat to them. Their opposition grew and they began to conspire among themselves against him. They openly discussed ways to get rid of him. The consequences of this increasing suspicion and bitterness led to Jesus' pointed accusation in the parables of the Two Sons and the Wicked Tenants. Realizing that Jesus' charge was directed against them, the chief priests and Pharisees began to look for ways to arrest him.

As Jesus taught in the temple, the Pharisees and Sadducees challenged his authority to teach and took turns challenging him on issues of the Jewish Law. Jesus' indictment reached a high point in his scathing denunciation of the scribes, Pharisees, and hypocrites with a series of woes pronounced against them.

Their plans to destroy Jesus culminated in their conspiracy with Judas to betray Jesus and Jesus' arrest in the Garden of Gethsemane. They tried Jesus for blasphemy before the Jewish court, suborning false testimony that he claimed to be the Son of God. Rendering a verdict of guilty, deserving a sentence of death, they sent him to the Roman governor, Pontius Pilate, to be tried. The animosity between Jesus and the Jewish authorities reached its highest point as they incited the crowds to seek Barabbas' release and demand Jesus' crucifixion. Pilate, fearing mob violence, condemned him to die, and he was crucified. Their plans to destroy Jesus had been successful.

Class Members — Preparation Guide

1. Using the resource sheets (pages 21 and 22), track the occasions when Jesus and the disciples seemed to be on different tracks.
   - What was their opposition to Jesus' plans?
   - What alternatives did they propose?
   - How did Jesus respond to their objections?

2. Trace the growing conflict between Jesus and Jewish authorities.
   - With a Bible dictionary, like *Harper's Bible Dictionary*, identify the different groups who opposed Jesus:
     — Scribes, Pharisees, Sadducees, Chief Priests, Elders, and Temple Authorities.
     — Who led the conspiracy to destroy Jesus?
     — From whom did Jesus seem most alienated?
   - Identify the points in the narrative at which the Jewish authorities increased the conflict with decisions to destroy Jesus.
   - Describe Jesus' response to the growing animosity.

3. Read the series of woes which Jesus pronounced against the Jewish leaders, Matthew 23:1-39.
   - Make a list of the six charges with which he accused them of hypocrisy.
     — With which charges can you most readily identify?
     — Which charges are most vague to you and difficult to apply?

Matthew's Extended Passion Narrative

Matthew introduces the three themes — Matthew 16:21-23

I. Predictions Of The Passion
First — 16:21
suffer, and be killed, but raised third day
Second — 17:22-23
delivered and be killed, and raised
Third — 20:17-19
delivered, condemned to death, crucified, and raised
Cf. 21:33-41
Parable of Wicked Tenants, who did not respect the owner's son, but killed him.
26:2 — Jesus predicted death

II. The Journey To Jerusalem
16:21 — He must go to Jerusalem
    17:1-9 — Mount of Transfiguration
    17:22 — a gathering in Galilee
    17:24 — in Capernaum
    19:1 — Left Galilee for Judea
20:18 — to go up to Jerusalem
In Jerusalem
21:1-11 — Triumphal Entry by Bethphage, and Mount of Olives
21:17 — Bethany
26:6 — Bethany

III. Increasing Isolation And Conflict
1. Isolation from the disciples
16:22-23 — Peter rebuked Jesus, Jesus reprimanded Peter
17:1-8 — Mount of Transfiguration, Peter proposed to stay
19:13-15 — Challenge over blessing children
20:20-28 — Debate over who is greatest
26:14-16, 20-25, 47-50 — Judas' betrayal
26:31-35, 69-75 — Peter's denial

26:36-46 — Disciples slept through Jesus' prayer
26:56 — Disciples deserted Jesus
2. Conflict with the Jewish leaders
    9:10-17, 32-34; 12:1-14, 38-45; 15:1-20; 16:1-12 — Earlier
      accounts of conflict
    16:21 — Great suffering at hands of elders, chief priests, scribes
    19:3-9 — Pharisees' challenge over marriage
    20:18-19 — Chief Priests, Scribes
    21:12-16 — Cleansing the Temple
    21:23-27 — Challenge over authority
    21:28-46 — Parables: Two Sons, Wicked Tenants
    22:15-46 — Challenges by Pharisees, Sadducees
    23:1-39 — Series of woes
    26:3-5 — Chief Priests, Scribes, Elders seek to kill him
    26:14-16 — Plot with Judas
    26:47-68 — Arrest and trial
    27:1-2 — Jesus delivered to Pilate
    27:20 — Chief Priests incited crowd
3. With The Crowds
    21:8-11 — Acclamations of praise
    27:15-26 — They demanded his death, asking for Barabbas

Group Leader —
Suggestions For Class Discussion

1. Matthew is often interpreted as the most Jewish of the Gospels. He includes in the section of Jesus' teaching in the temple legalistic debates with the Pharisees and Sadducees over interpretation of the Law and a lengthy denunciation of scribes and Pharisees in the pronouncement of woes. Mark has only a short passage of woes, and Luke includes this earlier on the road to Jerusalem. Discuss Matthew's interest in the Jewish Law. Why did he write so knowledgeably about Jewish customs? Why did he include details of Judaism that the other Gospels omitted? Was this most Jewish of Gospels written to a community of Christians converted from Judaism? Was Matthew forming a theological base for Jews to be faithful disciples of Christ?

2. You may wish to discuss the growing conflict with the Jewish authorities that led to Jesus' death. Trace the incidents and note how the conflict grew more intense. At which points did they want to be rid of Jesus? Or to destroy him?

3. Discuss the relationships between Jesus and the disciples through the journey to Jerusalem and during the last week. What were the tensions? Did the relationships among the disciples deteriorate? Did Jesus allow the stress to affect his relationship with them?

4. The animosity and conflict between Jesus and the Jewish authorities raises serious questions of toleration between religious groups of varying beliefs. You might discuss with the class principles of tolerance with persons whose faith and doctrine or whose religious practices differ from our own. There might be occasion to discuss religious pluralism in the twenty-first century.

Lesson 3

A Travel Narrative

Texts: Luke 9:51-62;   10:1, 38-42;   13:22-35;
                    14:25-33;   17:11-19;   18:31-43;
                    19:1-10;   19:11-27;   19:28-44

Themes: The Journey to Jerusalem
                    Lament for the Holy City

A Relentless Journey

The travel narrative of Jesus' journey to Jerusalem is the dominant feature of the Gospel of Luke. It is the longest section, Luke 9:51—19:48, emphasizing the progression toward the Holy City as Jesus drew ever nearer to his impending death. The compulsive character of the journey was set after Jesus' second prediction of the Passion (Luke 9:44), as Luke introduced the travel narrative with the solemn declaration, "When the days drew near for him to be taken up, he set his face to go to Jerusalem" (9:51). From this point on Jesus would not turn back. He was determined to go to Jerusalem even though he knew he would be arrested, tried, and executed in the city. Nothing the disciples could say or do could deter him. He would not heed even a warning by the Pharisees that Herod sought to kill him (13:31-33), insisting that it was his destiny to die in Jerusalem.

Twice on the journey Jesus wept in lamentation for the city. Toward the midpoint of Luke's account (13:33-35), just after the warning by the Pharisees not to go to Jerusalem, Jesus reminded them that the prophet was destined to die in Jerusalem, and lamented the fate of the city that kills its messengers from God. Second, the journey culminated in Jesus' lament as he approached the city on the Day of the Triumphal Entry. With the multitudes on the road proclaiming him king and shouting, "Blessed is the king who

25

comes in the name of the Lord," Jesus wept for the city (19:38, 41-44). It was a moment of high drama, an occasion for rejoicing and celebration. Yet, relentless in his resolve to reach Jerusalem, knowing it was there he would die, Jesus entered the city in sorrow and grief, not for himself, but for the holy city of God.

Travelogue

The framework of Luke's travel narrative is shaped by repeated notations describing Jesus' progress toward the Holy City. On six occasions — Luke 9:51-53; 13:22, 33-34; 17:11; 18:31-33; 19:11; 19:28, 41 — Luke specifically says Jesus was on the way, going up to Jerusalem. On five other occasions — Luke 10:1; 10:38; 14:25; 18:35; 19:1 — he adds comments on Jesus' itinerary. These notes are like pegs in the outline around which Luke composes his narrative.

The common pattern is to follow each episode with an interlude in which Luke includes material extraneous to the travel narrative. Some of this material Luke shares with Matthew, mostly out of sequence and generally found in Matthew's Galilean period. Very little of this material is found in Mark. Of the material found only in Luke the dominant passages are the familiar Lucan parables. Twelve parables peculiar to Luke are in the boundaries of the travel narrative, including the Good Samaritan, the Prodigal Son, the Unjust Steward, Dives and Lazarus, the Unjust Judge, and the Pharisee and Publican. Seven other parables are included which are also in Matthew. Three miracle stories of healing found only in Luke are included, plus one miracle also in Matthew and Mark. Two familiar meal narratives found only in Luke are included, the stories of Mary and Martha, and Zacchaeus, and there is a brief note of going to eat a meal with a leader of the Pharisees on the Sabbath.

Luke's Parable Collection

In the Synoptic Gospels, Jesus' favorite teaching method was by parables. There are 37 parables, or 39 if a couple with similar themes but different details are read as individual stories rather than doublets. Luke includes the most — 26, while Matthew has

22 and Mark has eight. Luke also has the most found only in one Gospel — thirteen, with nine peculiar to Matthew and two only in Mark.

The differences in use of the parables by Luke and Matthew are striking. In Luke, the parables are spread throughout the travel narrative. Of the total 26 in Luke, nineteen are in the travel narrative, with twelve of these only in Luke. A thirteenth, the Pounds, is similar to Matthew's parable of the Talents (Matthew 25:14-30), although the details are quite different. Luke uses the parables as teaching occasions on the journey to Jerusalem. On four occasions the parables lead into the itinerary note, i.e.: 1) 10:29-37, the Good Samaritan — 10:38, visit to Martha and Mary's home, 2) 13:18-21, Mustard Seed and Leaven — 13:22, Teaching on the way to Jerusalem, 3) 14:15-24, the Great Supper — 14:25, Crowds traveling with him, 4) 17:7-10, Faithful Servants — 17:11, On the way to Jerusalem. On one occasion the parable of the Pounds is the focus of the itinerary note, 19:11, "He went on to tell a parable because he was near Jerusalem."

In Matthew the parables are concentrated in three teaching collections: 1) Chapter 13, where the parable of the sower and seven parables of the Kingdom are gathered; 2) the Temple Teaching, chapters 21-22, with three parables; and 3) the Eschatological Discourse, chapters 24-25, with five parables. Matthew has eleven parables in the Galilean Ministry, only three on the journey to Jerusalem, and eight after the arrival in Jerusalem. Luke has only five in the Galilean ministry, nineteen in the Travel Narrative, and two after the arrival in Jerusalem. It seems evident that Luke's parable collection is predominantly in the Travel Narrative.

The greatest concentration of parables in Luke is in chapters 15-18, where eight parables are gathered. Seven of these are peculiar to Luke, with the only exception the parable of the Lost Sheep, which Luke shares with Matthew.

The character of the parables is also different. In Matthew eleven are parables of the Kingdom. Only four of Luke's parables might be classified in this genre. Eight of Matthew's parables are simple comparisons of likeness, while only four of Luke's are of this form.

Most of Luke's parables, especially those peculiar to Luke, are stories related to teach lessons of human nature and ethical behavior. Paranetic in character, they illustrate examples of compassion for the poor, the outcasts, and the marginal, exhortations of personal behavior, and principles of spiritual discipline. Jesus told them to instruct the hearers in righteousness and to show what God expects of the chosen people in their personal lives. The parables were Jesus' most profound teaching on discipleship.

Class Members — Preparation Guide

1. Track the journey of Jesus to Jerusalem through the lesson texts. For each stage of the journey
- Find Luke's notation of Jesus' resolve to go to Jerusalem,
- List what happens at each stage, and
- Identify the various types of stories:
  i.e. narratives of events, miracle stories, parables, teaching stories.

2. Compare Luke's laments for the city (Luke 13:34-35 and 19:41-44) with Matthew's lament (Matthew 23:37-39). Luke's first lamentation is almost identical to Matthew's. The second is a new lamentation, joined with the earlier lament by the acclamation of beatitude shouted by the crowds during the triumphant ride into Jerusalem.

What common elements do you find in the three lamentations?

3. Read and meditate on the favorite Lucan parables:
- The Good Samaritan, 10:25-37
- The Rich Fool, 12:13-21
- The Lost Sheep and the Lost Coin, 15:3-10
- The Prodigal Son, or the Two Sons, 15:11-32
- The Unjust Steward, 16:1-9
- Dives and Lazarus, 16:19-31
- The Unjust Judge, 18:1-8
- The Pharisee and the Publican, 18:9-14.

For each write a brief sentence on what you think the parable teaches.

Luke's Travel Narrative

1. Luke 9:51 — **Introduction To The Narrative**
   "He set his face to go to Jerusalem."
   > Cf. 9:53 — "Because his face was set toward Jerusalem."
   > 9:52-56 — "They entered a village of the Samaritans ... they went on to another village."
   > 9:57-62 — "As they were going along the road." Excuses for failing to follow Jesus

   Interlude — 10:1-37
   Mission of the Seventy to the towns he intended to visit
   The Great Commandment — Parable of the Good Samaritan*

2. Luke 10:38-42 — **Journey Resumed**
   "As they went on their way, he entered a certain village." Visit to the home of Mary and Martha*

   Interlude — 11:1—13:21
   Material shared with Matthew, mostly from the Galilean ministry.
   > The Lord's Prayer, "Ask and it will be given...." Miracle of casting out a demon and the Beelzebub controversy, Teaching and aphorisms collected by Matthew in the sermon on the mount, signs of this evil generation, woes pronounced against the Pharisees (Cf. Matthew 23), Parables of the Owner and Slaves, the Mustard Seed, and Leaven.

   Material peculiar to Luke
   • Parables: the Friend at Midnight*, the Rich Man*, Fruitless Fig Tree*
   • Miracle: Healing a woman with an infirmity*
   • Teaching: A call to repentance*

3. Luke 13:22-35 — **Teaching In The Villages**
   "Through one town and village after another, teaching as he made his way to Jerusalem."
   > 10:22-30 — A Condemnation of Israel — the first will be last and the last first.

10:31-33 — Warning by the Pharisees that Herod sought to kill him. "I must be on my way, because it is impossible for a prophet to be killed outside of Jerusalem."
10:34-35 — Lament for the Holy City — "Jerusalem, Jerusalem, the city that kills the prophets."

Interlude — 14:1-24
Dinner with a Pharisee, Healing a man with dropsy*
Teaching on Humility*, Parable of the Great Supper

4. Luke 14:25-35 — **Journey Resumed**
"Large crowds were traveling with him." Teaching on the Cost of Discipleship

Interlude — 15:1—17:10
A Collection of Parables: The Lost Sheep (with Matthew), Lost Coin*, Prodigal Son*, Unjust Steward*, Dives and Lazarus*, Treatment of a Servant*
Challenge to the Pharisees, Debate on Law and Divorce, Teaching on Offending Children, Forgiveness, and Faith

5. Luke 17:11-19 — **Through Samaria And Galilee**
"On the way to Jerusalem" Miracle: Healing Ten Lepers*

Interlude — 17:20—18:30
Parables: the Unjust Judge*, the Pharisee and Publican*
Teaching on the Kingdom of God and the Day of the Son of Man
Receiving Children and the Rich Young Ruler (with Matthew and Mark)

6. Luke 18:31-34 — **Third Prediction Of The Passion**
"Going up to Jerusalem"

Luke 18:35-43 — **Road To Jericho**
"As he approached Jericho" — Miracle: Healing a blind man

7. Luke 19:1-10 — **Jericho**
"He entered Jericho and was passing through it." Dinner with Zacchaeus*

8. Luke 19:11-27 — **Teaching**
  "Because he was near Jerusalem" — Parable of the Pounds

9. Luke 19:28-44 — **Triumphal Entry**
  "He went on ahead, going up to Jerusalem."
    19:28-40 — Triumphal Entry to the Holy City
    19:41-44 — Lament for Jerusalem — "As he came near
    and saw the city, he wept over it."

*Material only in Luke

Group Leader —
Suggestions For Class Discussion

1. Luke's Gospel structure using a lengthy Travel Narrative is paralleled in part in the second volume of his work, the history of the early church in Acts.

   Luke
   1-2 — The Birth of Jesus
   4—9:50 — Short Ministry of Jesus and the Disciples in Galilee
   9:51—19:44 — Travel Narrative: Jesus' Journey to Jerusalem
   19:45—23:56 — Jerusalem, culminating in the Passion, Death and Burial

   Acts
   1-2 — The Birth of the Church
   3-8; 10-12 — Short Ministry of the Disciples in Judea and Samaria
   13—28:15 — Travel Narrative: Paul's Mission and Journey to Rome
   28:16-31 — Rome, with Paul in prison.

   Explore with the class why Luke shows such interest in the Travel Narrative. Was he, a person from the world outside the Holy Land, more knowledgeable and interested in the mobility of the first century? Was he writing for a community of faith outside the Holy Land? Is this why his concern for the early church's mission comes to the fore? Was he breaking the gospel loose from its Jewish boundaries for a world of the Diaspora?

2. Luke's use of parables offers the class almost unlimited possibilities for study and discussion. Include in the class discussion at least the parables of the Good Samaritan, the Prodigal Son, and, because of its focus on Jesus' impending death, the parable of the Wicked Tenants.

3. The lengthy Travel Narrative as an expansion of the Passion theme anticipates the interpretation of the Passion story as a model of Christian discipleship. After the first prediction of the Passion in Luke 9:22-27, Luke introduces the thought of taking up one's cross daily and following Jesus. The lessons and parables of the Travel Narrative explore the meaning of discipleship as sharing with Jesus in his suffering and death. Discuss with the class what they teach about discipleship.

Lesson 4

A Holy Week In Jerusalem

Texts: Matthew 21:1-13; Mark 11:1-19; Luke 19:28-46
            Luke 19:47-48; 21:37-38
            Matthew 21:23—24:1

Themes: Jesus' Last Week
            The Triumphal Entry into Jerusalem
            Days of Teaching in the Temple

Riding To A Coronation

Jesus' last week began with a Triumphal Entry into the Holy
City. He rode a donkey along the road from Jericho, via Bethphage
and Bethany, passing by the Mount of Olives with its sinister anticipation of his Passion. It was a festive parade, with crowds lin-
ing the roadway, shouting and acclaiming him king, praising the
One who came in the name of the Lord.

The narratives of Jesus' triumphant ride are familiar. The details of his instructions to the disciples to secure a donkey upon
which to ride, of the disciples spreading their cloaks on its back for
Jesus to sit, of the crowds throwing their cloaks on the road and
ripping branches from the bushes by the roadside to form a royal
carpet are well-known. The anthems of praise sung by the multitudes proclaim him king. In Matthew the acclamation reflects the
prophecy of Zechariah 9:9. The doxology, "Blessed is the One who
comes in the name of the Lord," echoes Jesus' lament for Jerusalem (Matthew 23:37-39 // Luke 13:34-35).

The irony of Jesus' entry into the Holy City is startling. The
week began with the crowds acclaiming him king. It would end
with them demanding his death. It began with them singing,
"Blessed is the One who comes in the name of the Lord," and
"Hosanna in the highest heaven." It would end with them mocking
and taunting and deriding and cursing him as he hung on the cross.

It began with the disciples spreading their cloaks for a royal saddle, strewing branches to form a royal road. It would end with them deserting him in his moment of distress, running away in fear and despair. In his last week he went from coronation to crucifixion, from sovereign Lord to servant, from triumph to despair. But through it all, he remained a king, the King of the Jews, and the King of Kings.

Cleansing The Temple

Jesus' first action in the city was to visit the temple where he drove out the moneychangers and merchants selling animals for sacrifice. Jesus was an angry young man, incensed at the commercial exploitation and spiritual corruption of the worship of God. Cleansing the temple was a preparation for Jesus' ministry of teaching in the temple through the first days of Holy Week. It was a purification of the holy place where Jesus taught the Word of God. His action infuriated the Jewish leaders who intensified their efforts to arrest and destroy him.

Mark has a different timing for the temple cleansing. All three Gospels report that Jesus went directly to the temple at the conclusion of the triumphal ride into the city. Matthew and Luke indicate that the cleansing of the temple took place at this time, on the first day of the week, but Mark says that Jesus merely looked around and then returned to Bethany to spend the night. The temple cleansing took place the following morning when he returned to the city.

Jesus' Ministry Of Teaching

Teaching dominated the first days of the week. Each day Jesus came to the temple in Jerusalem to teach; each evening he returned to Bethany to spend the night and sleep.

In Luke 19:47-48 and 21:37-38 is a literary style known as an "inclusivo," a beginning and end. It is a preface and a summary to the days in Jerusalem. Luke uses the same clause to introduce and to bring to a close the teaching ministry: "Every day he was teaching in the temple." In both references Luke calls attention to the crowds who came to hear him teach. They were spellbound with his wisdom and authority.

36

Matthew And The Teaching Collection

Matthew gathered Jesus' temple teaching in an extended discourse, seeming to treat it as a major teaching collection in the Gospel, comparable to the Sermon on the Mount, chapters 5-7, or the Discourse on Discipleship, chapter 18. He appears to be caught in a dilemma. There are five primary addresses or discourses in Matthew. Each ends with a formal conclusion, either, "When Jesus had finished saying these things, he left Galilee" (7:28; 19:1; 26:1), or "When Jesus had finished instructing his twelve disciples, he went on from there to teach," or "finished these parables, he left that place" (11:1; 13:53).

1) 5-7 — Sermon on the Mount, ending with 7:28
2) 10 — Mission Discourse, ending with 11:1
3) 13 — Parables of the Kingdom, ending with 13:53
4) 18 — Discipleship Discourse, ending with 19:1
5) 24-25 — The Gospel Apocalypse, ending with 26:1

It has long been thought that Matthew was reflecting the Five Books of the Torah with the five discourses. If he were to consider the temple teaching as a primary discourse, they would add up to six and lose the symbolism of the five books of Moses. Yet Matthew wanted to emphasize the temple teaching. He closed it with a formula saying, "As Jesus came out of the temple and was going away" (24:1). It sounds very similar to the five repeated formulae after each of the five discourses. It is just different enough to show that Matthew doesn't want to add to the five discourses, and thus omits the formula, "He *finished these sayings*," but is just similar enough to heighten his emphasis on the temple teaching.

Increasing Conflict

The primary focus of the temple teaching in Matthew is the growing conflict between Jesus and the Jewish leaders. The Temple Cleansing introduces the theme. It is followed by miracles of healing the blind and the lame, which further infuriated the chief priests and scribes. They complained because children were singing praise to Jesus.

When Jesus returned to the temple the following morning, the chief priests and elders challenged his authority to teach. In response, Jesus told the parables of the Two Sons and the Wicked Tenants. Realizing that Jesus was verbally attacking them, the chief priests and Pharisees stepped up their attempts to arrest Jesus. The main body of the temple teaching consists of legal debates between Jesus and the Jewish leaders over the meaning of the Law — TORAH. The Pharisees and Sadducees took turns challenging Jesus, and Jesus responded by challenging them. The high point of the conflict was Jesus' scathing denunciation of the scribes, Pharisees, and hypocrites in pronouncing six woes for failure to honor and respect the Law.

Class Members — Preparation Guide

1. Read the parallel accounts of the Triumphal Entry
   Matthew 21:1-11; Mark 11:1-11; Luke 19:28-44
   • What similarities can you identify?
   • What differences are there in the three accounts?

2. Compare Matthew 21:10-17; Mark 11:11-19; and Luke 19:45-48.
   How does Mark's account differ from the reports of Matthew and Luke?

3. In Matthew 21:23-27, read the Pharisees' challenge made against Jesus' authority to teach.
   • How did Jesus answer their challenge?
   • What was their response?
   • Compare Jesus' challenge to the scribes and Pharisees in Matthew 23:1-10.
   • Of what did Jesus accuse them?
   • Who was the one teacher to whom Jesus referred?
   • What did Jesus mean by this claim?

4. Using the resource sheet on the temple teaching (pages 40-41) quickly read through the parables and sayings of Jesus in one of the Gospels. Trace the references to Jesus as a teacher and note the themes about which he taught.

The Temple Teaching

	Matthew	Mark	Luke
1. Introducing the days in Jerusalem	21:14-17	11:11	19:47-48
Each day he taught in the temple	21:23		19:47
Crowds were amazed at his teaching		11:18	19:48
2. Debate over Authority to teach	21:23-27	11:27-33	20:1-8
3. Parable of Two Sons	21:28-32		
4. Parable of Wicked Tenants	21:33-44	12:1-11	20:9-18
5. Parable of the Marriage Feast	22:1-14		(14:15-24)
6. Taxes and Tribute to Caesar	22:15-22	12:13-17	20:20-26
Pharisees called him "Teacher"	22:16	12:14	20:21
7. Question concerning Resurrection	22:23-33	12:18-27	20:27-40
Sadducees called him "Teacher"	22:24	12:19	20:28
Crowds astounded at his teaching	22:33		
A Scribe called him "Teacher"			20:39
8. The Great Commandment	22:34-40	12:28-34	(10:25-28)
A Lawyer called him "Teacher"	22:35-36		
A Scribe called him "Teacher"		12:32	(10:25)
9. Question about the Messiah	22:41-46	12:35-37a	20:41-44
Jesus taught in the temple		12:35	
10. Woes pronounced against Pharisees	23:1-36	12:37b-40	20:45-47
Jesus was teaching		12:38	
Jesus called himself one teacher	23:8-10		
11. Lament for Jerusalem	23:37-39		(13:34-35; 19:41-44)
12. The Widow's Mite		12:41-44	21:1-4
13. Predicting Destruction of the Temple	24:1-2	13:1-2	21:5-7
14. The Synoptic Apocalypse	24:3-42	13:3-37	21:8-36

Group Leader —
Suggestions For Class Discussion

1. Explore with the class the Pharisee's challenge to Jesus' authority to teach (Matthew 21:23-27) and Jesus' challenge to the scribes and Pharisees (Matthew 23:1-10).
   - What were the issues of conflict between them?
   - Note Jesus' commendation of the Pharisees' teaching, but his warning against their hypocrisy in acting out what they said.
   - How did Jesus feel about his role as a teacher?

2. Jesus' temple teaching offers many possibilities for class discussion.
   - Select one of the parables to study with the class. The parable of the Wedding Feast, Matthew 22:1-14, might be appropriate, since it is not discussed in another lesson in these studies.
   - Discuss the teaching of the Great Commandment, Matthew 22:34-40. Explore with the class ways the Great Commandment informs our ethics for the new century. Ask them to share ways they feel it helps them in their own personal behavior.
   - Discuss the story of the Widow's Mite, Mark 12:41-44 and Luke 21:1-4. Compare this stewardship lesson with Jesus' teaching on tithing, Matthew 23:23-24.

Lesson 5

A Last Supper In The Upper Room

Texts: Matthew 26:1-30; Mark 14:1-26; Luke 22:1-39
            Cf. Exodus 12:1-27; 13:3-10

Themes: Jesus' Last Supper with the Disciples
            Passover and Seder Meal
            Preparing for Jesus' Death

Preparing For The Passion

Allusions to the impending death of Jesus dominate the narratives surrounding the last evening he spent with the disciples before his arrest. Calling the disciples' attention to the approaching Passover, in Matthew Jesus announced his expected crucifixion. The Passover-Seder Meal itself was a remembrance of the Israelite exodus from Egypt. Repeated each year on the night of Passover, it recalled the slaying of the sacrificial lamb, whose blood was spread on the lintels of the houses of the Israelites as a sign for the angel of death to pass over that house. Jesus was understood to be the Lamb of God, slain for the redemption of God's people. During the supper, Jesus revealed the conspiracy betraying him into the hands of the Jewish authorities. In distributing the bread and wine Jesus alluded twice to his death.

Anointing Jesus For His Death

Between Jesus' first notice of the approaching Passover and his instructions to the disciples to prepare for the meal, Matthew 26:6-13 and Mark 14:3-9 insert the narrative of a woman who anointed Jesus' head with costly ointment. Luke 7:36-50 reported a similar incident, but at a different time, with different details and theme. Matthew and Mark included the story as an anticipation of Jesus' death.

43

Jesus had returned to Bethany to spend the night. He was eating at the home of Simon the leper when a woman came into the house and poured an alabaster jar of costly ointment on his head. The disciples objected vociferously over such an expensive waste, but Jesus reprimanded them, saying she had prepared his body for burial. Perhaps he realized that after his death there would not be enough time before the beginning of the Sabbath to prepare his body properly with spices and ointments.

Conspiracy And Betrayal

The conflict between Jesus and the Jewish authorities had reached its climax. Their challenges to his temple teaching had all been repulsed and dismissed. The crowds were still astonished at his teaching and remained supportive. Convinced that they had no further recourse, and determined to be rid of him, in desperation they conspired to find some way to arrest and kill him. Afraid to seize him publicly, because the crowds were with him, they feared a riot. The three synoptic accounts vary in their details, but all three emphasize this final effort to destroy Jesus. Matthew has the most detailed account, reporting that the chief priests and elders met in the palace residence of Caiaphas, the high priest.

The Jewish leaders got a favorable break when one of the twelve disciples, Judas Iscariot, decided to betray Jesus. Agreeing to sell Jesus out to them for a payment of money, he began to look for a suitable opportunity to turn Jesus over to them, trying to find a time when Jesus would not be accompanied by the crowds.

The Evening Meal — The Last Supper

During the meal Jesus announced that one of the twelve would betray him, but he did not reveal to the group which one it would be. They were deeply distressed and confused, asking who it might be. Only Matthew tells us that Jesus confided to Judas that Jesus knew it was he.

There has been much discussion over the character of this last supper with the disciples. All three Synoptic Gospels make very clear that it was the Passover Meal, on the evening of the day the sacrificial lamb was killed. The identification of Jesus as the sacrificial Lamb of God, who willingly gave his life for the deliverance of God's chosen people from the bondage of their sin is at the heart of the supper. Breaking and distributing the loaf of bread to them, he interpreted it as his body. Passing the cup of wine to them, he interpreted it as his blood of the new covenant, poured out for the forgiveness of sin. From beginning to end the meal was overshadowed by the dark clouds of Jesus' rapidly approaching death.

The Lord's Supper

The Sacrament of Holy Communion, or the Lord's Supper, is the most liturgically profound and theologically significant occasion of worship for the Christian Church. From the Roman Catholic Mass to the simple shared meal of a house church; from the priestly consecrated elements of Episcopal churches to the common bread and grape juice of Presbyterian and Baptist churches; from the liturgical observance of Lutheran churches to the spontaneous prayers of congregational churches, the sacrament is the highest moment of worship for people gathered to remember the sacrificial death of Jesus Christ for our salvation.

Jesus instituted the sacrament in the Upper Room at his Last Supper with the disciples, instructing them to repeat it, "Do this in remembrance of me" (Luke 22:19). From that moment on the Lord's Supper has been the epitome of Christian worship.

The sacrament is a meal of remembrance. It recalls the death of Christ by which we are saved. The bread, symbolizing the body of Jesus broken for us, and the cup, symbolizing the blood of Christ shed for the remission of our sins, allow us to relive his sacrifice to redeem us. But it is no sad and morose occasion. It is the experience of our highest joy, for it leads us to renew our faith in Jesus Christ, the Lamb of God, the Son of God crucified for us, which is God's gift to save us.

Class Members — Preparation Guide

1. The Conspiracy Formula

Compare Luke 19:47-48 with Luke 22:2; then with Matthew 26:3-5 and Mark 14:1-2. Luke includes the conspiracy formula both before and after the temple teaching. See also Matthew 21:46 // Mark 12:12 // Luke 20:19 where the formula follows Jesus' parable of the Wicked Tenants and repeats the Jewish leaders' reluctance to arrest Jesus openly because they were afraid of his popularity with the crowds.

Matthew 26:2 uses the occasion of announcing the coming Passover for Jesus to predict his approaching crucifixion. Mark 14:1 and Luke 22:1 simply announce that the Festival of Unleavened Bread — Passover is near.

2. Preparations For The Passover Meal

Read in order Matthew 26:17-19; Mark 14:12-16; Luke 22:7-13. Matthew is the shortest. What other details are included in Mark? What did Luke add?

Read Moses' instructions on observance of Passover, Exodus 12:1-27; 13:3-10.

3. The Last Supper

Read the parallel accounts, Matthew 26:20-30; Mark 14:17-26; Luke 22:14-23.

Make a list of what happened in each account.

- What is included in all three narratives? What differences can you find?
- If we had only the accounts of Matthew and Mark, what would we miss?

Read Paul's account of the Institution of the Lord's Supper, 1 Corinthians 11:23-26.

- Which of the Gospel accounts did Paul follow most closely?
- What did Paul add?

Group Leader —
Suggestions For Class Discussion

1. **A Wasteful Gesture Or An Act Of Ministry**

    The episode of the woman who anointed Jesus with an expensive ointment might give you an opportunity to discuss with the class stewardship policy on how to choose priorities in the use of church resources. The disciples challenged her act as a wasteful gesture. The money could have been used to help the poor. Explore the common arguments used in the church to justify large amounts spent for current expenses, or to operate the program of the church. Or discuss the large expenditures for capital building funds, used to construct church facilities. What arguments are made to use church funds for mission projects, or to help the poor, or to support social action agencies and programs? How do we make wise choices in the use of church funds?

2. **Passover — Seder — Lord's Supper**

    We have begun to see the observance of "the Seder" or "Christian Seder" in churches during Holy Week. It dramatizes the experience of Jesus with the disciples in the Upper Room at the Last Supper, and recalls the Passover Meal, which was the occasion for this Last Supper. You might spend some time in class discussing the Jewish Seder Meal and how we might reenact this occasion with dignity and without disparaging or misusing this most significant of Jewish rituals. What liturgy might we use? What day of Holy Week would be most appropriate? Would it be proper to substitute a Seder Meal for the Sacrament of Holy Communion on Maundy Thursday?

3. **The Lord's Supper**

    This theme also gives you the opportunity to discuss the meaning of the Lord's Supper and how we observe this most significant of Christian rituals. What is the character of the meal? Is it a sad occasion in remembrance of Jesus' death? Or is it a joyous occasion for Jesus' gift of salvation? You might also explore the varied rubrics and practices by which different denominations observe the Lord's Supper. Discuss the distribution of only bread, the common cup, the intinction method, service by the celebrant, or service by elders, service in the pews, or the congregation coming to a kneeling bench. What churches have closed communion? What churches have open communion? You can think of other issues. What do the different practices signify?

Lesson 6

Gethsemane And
A Sentence Of Death

Texts: Matthew 26:30—27:26; Mark 14:26—15:15;
           Luke 22:39—23:25

Themes: Jesus' prayer in the garden
           Betrayal and Arrest
           The trials of Jesus

Jesus And The Disciples — Prayer In The Garden

The ominous specter of impending death continued to shadow the narratives of Jesus' last night. Stories of his anguished prayer in the garden, his arrest and trials before the Sanhedrin and Pontius Pilate never strayed far from the crucifixion awaiting Jesus.

From the Upper Room Jesus led the disciples to a secluded spot in the Garden of Gethsemane to pray. The brief, quiet retreat for spiritual strength prepared him for the ordeal of the Passion. Luke emphasizes the spiritual benefit, reporting that an angel from heaven appeared and gave him strength. The Gospels differ in details of the story, but all describe Jesus' anguished prayer for deliverance, demonstrating both his humanity and his divinity. He pled for God to deliver him, asking if it were possible that he be spared from drinking the bitter cup. It was an honest prayer. He wanted to escape the suffering. Nevertheless he submitted himself totally to God's will. He was to the end the obedient Son, the human who came into the world to do the divine will.

It is common in devotional reflections on this passage to focus on Jesus' submission to God's plan, in his petition, "Not my will, but thine be done." However, affirming the perfect obedience of the Son to the Father, we should not lose sight of Jesus' agony and torment, in the plea, "If it is possible, let this cup pass by me."

49

Luke especially describes Jesus' anguish, telling us his sweat fell to the ground as great drops of blood.

Nor should we miss the symbol of desertion by the disciples. Although Jesus implored them to watch with him and pray, they abandoned him to his lonely ordeal by falling asleep. Reflecting his prediction as they left the Upper Room that all would desert him, this occasion in the garden anticipates their frightened desertion at his arrest.

Jesus And Peter — Denial And Desertion

The stark contrast between Peter's courage in promising to support Jesus even to death, and his cowardice in denying he even knew Jesus is startling. It illustrates his humanity and demonstrates both his strength and weakness. He was big and strong, a fisherman by trade, accustomed to taking matters into his own hands and bending the will of others to his own wishes. Impetuous by character, and courageous by nature, he customarily acted out his first impulse and thought about it later. His spiritual and moral strength matched his physical strength. He was a natural leader, charismatic in style and unhesitant in assuming a leadership role. It was therefore totally in character for him to presume a stance of protecting Jesus from any threat or danger. But he was unable to control his own fear, and when confronted by the real threat his courageous resolve wilted, and he succumbed into the three-fold denial. Luke reports that at the moment of the third denial, when the cock crowed, Jesus turned and looked at Peter. It was the lowest point of Peter's life.

Peter's denial is a specific example anticipating the general desertion of all the disciples. Jesus predicted that all would desert him. They all professed their allegiance, but when he was arrested, they all fled.

Jesus And Judas — Betrayal And Arrest

At the Last Supper, Jesus had predicted that one of the disciples would betray him. Although all three Gospels include the conspiracy of Judas with the Jewish leaders, agreeing to betray

50

Jesus, only in Matthew was Judas named at the supper as the one. Also, only Matthew later reported Judas' suicide.

Judas had conspired to betray Jesus with a kiss. Matthew and Mark report that in the Garden of Gethsemane, Judas approached Jesus and kissed him, but in Luke Jesus stopped him before the kiss.

The arrest of Jesus was a violent occasion. One of the disciples cut off the ear of the high priest's slave. None of the Synoptic Gospels names the servant or reports which disciple it was. John tells us that Peter was the disciple, and the servant was Malchus. Only Luke tells us that Jesus healed the man's ear.

Jesus did not resist the arrest. He surrendered willingly to the authorities, voluntarily submitting himself to God's plan. He acted out the prayer in Gethsemane that God's will be done. When he was arrested, all the disciples fled, as he had predicted.

The Trials Of Jesus

The Gospels report two separate trials, first by the Jewish authorities, and second by the Roman governor. It is thought that the Jewish court could declare Jesus deserving of death, but they did not have the legal authority to execute a criminal. Therefore it was necessary for them to hand Jesus over to the Romans for execution.

Jesus And The Jews — Trial Before The Sanhedrin

Matthew demonstrates his familiarity with Jewish law and gives more details of the Jewish trial. He informs us that two corroborating witnesses were required to bring a charge against the accused. He tells us that the trial was held before the whole council, the Sanhedrin, and that the high priest was Caiaphas. Mark's account is similar. Both indicate that the first hearing was late in the evening after Jesus' arrest, and that the council reconvened in the morning to sentence him to death. Luke's account is the shortest. He reports that the trial took place the following morning.

The Jewish leaders tried to secure false testimony to convict Jesus. Jesus was first accused of claiming power to destroy the holy temple, predicting that he would rebuild it in three days. This recalls his prediction of the destruction of the temple, at the beginning of the Gospel Apocalypse — Matthew 24:1-2; Mark 13:1-2; Luke 21:5-6. The testimony was vague and confused, and the council could reach no verdict on this indictment.

The high priest then asked Jesus if he claimed to be the Messiah. Mark has a significant variation at this point, reporting that Jesus answered unequivocally, "I am." Matthew and Luke report a more restrained response, "You have said I am." Jesus added an apocalyptic reference to the Son of Man seated at the right hand of power, coming with the clouds of heaven. The high priest accused Jesus of blasphemy, claiming to be the promised Messiah and Son of God. Ranting and raving, tearing his judicial robes, and ruling that no further testimony was necessary he incited the council to convict Jesus and declare that he deserved to die. They handed him over to the Roman court.

Jesus And The Romans — The Trial Before Pilate
Luke's account of the Roman trial includes a separate hearing before Herod not mentioned in either Matthew or Mark. Matthew includes separate, personal details on Pilate's role.

The Jewish authorities accused Jesus of sedition against the Roman government. Luke describes the indictment, listing the charges against Jesus.
1) Subversion against the Jewish nations
2) Counseling non-payment of taxes to the Roman government
3) Claiming to be a king
4) Inciting a riot by his teaching

The indictment adds up to an accusation that Jesus was planning a coup d' etat to overthrow the rightful Roman government, organizing a rebellion, declaring himself King of the Jews, and setting up an alternative government. In the tense political situation the threat of revolution was very real to the Roman occupying forces. Pilate was sensitive to the danger. He immediately seized the accusation that Jesus claimed to be King of the Jews, and asked if it were true. Jesus refused to answer directly.

Pilate fully understood the accusation by the Jewish leaders and their motivation for seeking Jesus' death. He made repeated attempts to release Jesus, declaring that he found no validity to their claims and pronouncing Jesus innocent.

Matthew reports that Pilate's wife warned him to have nothing to do with Jesus' trial. Symbolically trying to show Jesus' innocence, Pilate washed his hands, declaring that he had no responsibility for the unlawful death.

Luke reports another attempt to judge Jesus innocent. Learning that Jesus was from Galilee, Pilate sent Jesus to be tried by Herod. Even in the face of vehement denunciations by the chief priests and scribes, Herod also declared Jesus undeserving of a sentence of death.

Pilate's attempt to free Jesus culminated in Barabbas' commuted sentence. It was customary for the Roman governor to declare clemency for a criminal during the festival. Pilate attempted to set Jesus free, but the crowds demanded instead the release of Barabbas, a convicted murderer and revolutionary. It is ironic to note the mob violence of the scene. The Jewish leaders incited the crowds to demand Jesus' crucifixion. Accusing Jesus of inciting a riot, they used a riot to demand his death. The crowds, who had proclaimed him king at the beginning of the week, in the triumphal procession into the city, and who had been astonished at his teaching in the temple all week long, spontaneously turned against him, and demanded that Pilate deliver him to be killed. The Jewish authorities, who had been afraid to act publicly against Jesus because of his popularity with the crowds, now used the crowds, manipulating them to achieve their goal of Jesus' death.

The consequence was that Pilate, the powerful Roman governor, was powerless before the mob, and sentenced Jesus to be crucified.

Class Members — Preparation Guide

1. Gethsemane
Compare Matthew 26:36-46 with Luke 22:39-46.
- How does Luke's account differ?
- How did the disciples respond to Jesus' ordeal?
- For what did Jesus pray?

Withdrawal into the quiet discipline of prayer prepares us for difficult times. Prayer is a devotional exercise for spiritual strength. Think of occasions in your life when quiet moments of prayer have given you strength and faith.

2. The Trials Of Jesus
Read Matthew's account of the Jewish trial, Matthew 26:57-68; 27:1-2.
- What charges did the Jews make against Jesus? How did Jesus respond?
- What rule governing witnesses' testimony does Matthew demonstrate?
- Of what indictment did the Jewish Council convict Jesus?
- What sentence did the Council decree?

Read Luke's account of the Roman trial, Luke 23:1-25.
- With what indictment did the Jewish Council turn Jesus over to Pontius Pilate?
- Of what did Pilate accuse Jesus? How did Jesus respond to Pilate's accusation?
- Why did Pilate send Jesus to Herod? What was the result of the trial by Herod?
- What efforts did Pilate make to release Jesus?
- What sentence did Pilate decree against Jesus?

Group Leader —
Suggestions For Class Discussion

1. The possibilities for class discussion in this lesson are limitless. Consider a character study of the principal characters.

   Compare Judas Iscariot and Simon Peter and their roles in the story of Jesus' arrest and trial. Jesus predicted both Judas' betrayal and Peter's denial.
   - How did each react to Jesus' prediction?
   - Why did Judas decide to betray Jesus?
   - What caused Peter to deny Jesus?
   - How did Jesus react to Judas' betrayal and Peter's denial?

   Compare the judicial roles of the High Priest Caiaphas, the Galilean tetrarch Herod, and the Roman governor Pontius Pilate.
   - How did each exercise his legal authority?
   - What was each trying to achieve?
   - What was at stake for each?
   - How did each behave in performance of his duty?
   - What was the result of each trial?

2. Discuss Jesus' experience praying in the Garden of Gethsemane.
   - What does it reveal about the character of Jesus?
   - What does it say about the disciples?
   - How did it benefit Jesus?

3. Explore prayer as a spiritual discipline.
   - How does the practice of prayer give us strength?
   - On what occasions should we pray? How should we pray?

Lesson 7

He Was Crucified, Dead, And Buried

Texts: Matthew 27:24-66; Mark 15:15-47;
           Luke 23:24-56

Themes: The Road to Calvary
           Crucifixion and Death on the Cross
           The Burial of Jesus

Via Crucis — Via Dolorosa

The road that took Jesus from his conviction and sentence to death, in the court of Pontius Pilate, through his crucifixion, to his burial in the tomb of Joseph of Arimathea, was a trail of suffering and sorrow. The way of the cross was a road of pain and grief. Along the way were many characters.

- Pilate, who sentenced Jesus to death and ordered him to be flogged;
- Soldiers, who mocked and taunted Jesus, and put a crown of thorns on his head;
- An unfortunate bystander, Simon of Cyrene, who was forced to carry Jesus' cross;
- A group of women, forever known as the daughters of Jerusalem, who mourned Jesus' fate;
- The execution squad, who crucified Jesus and gambled for his clothing;
- The Jewish leaders and crowds, who derided him;
- Two criminals, who were crucified with Jesus;
- A centurion, who confessed Jesus' divine sonship;
- Joseph, who asked for Jesus' body, and buried him;
- Women disciples, including Mary Magdalene and Mary, the mother of Joseph, who followed the funeral procession to see where he was buried; and
- A military guard, who sealed and watched over the tomb.

It was an assembly of people experiencing the full, vast spectrum of human emotions, from the joyful celebration of the chief priests and elders, relieved and glad to be rid of Jesus, to the sad, quiet pathos of Mary Magdalene and the other Mary, their hearts broken, preparing for the last burial rights. There was the pathetic posturing of Pilate, trying to excuse himself for what he knew was a miscarriage of justice, and the ribald mocking of the Praetorian Guard. There was the indifference of the Roman soldiers, simply going through the motions, obeying the commands, crucifying him and casting lots for his robe, and the resentment of Simon at being forced to carry the cross. There was the mournful spectacle of the women who wept for him, and the fascinated hilarity of the crowd who had gathered to watch the crucifixion. There was the derision of one thief and the repentance of the other. There was the fear of the disciples who ran away, and the defeated resignation of Joseph, who saw his hopes dashed. And there was Jesus, Son of God, and King of the Jews, quietly, patiently, willingly enduring the jeers and derision, the excruciating pain, the loneliness, and isolation.

In The Chambers Of The Praetorian Guard

Only Matthew reports that when Pilate gave in to the demands of the crowd and sentenced Jesus to die, he tried to absolve himself of guilt for Jesus' wrongful death by publicly washing his hands. Pilate turned Jesus over to the guards, who made spite of their prisoner, mocking and taunting him. Laughing at the indictment of claiming to be King of the Jews, they fashioned a crown of thorns and crushed it down on his head. They gave him a reed for a kingly scepter, and clothed him in a royal robe (scarlet in Matthew, purple in Mark), and bowed down before him in derision. Jesus endured the indignity of being spat upon and whipped with the reed. Then, tiring of their childish play, the soldiers redressed him in his own robes and led him away to be crucified.

On The Road To Calvary

Two events occurred along the path. Simon of Cyrene, a visitor to Jerusalem for the festival, was seized out of the crowds standing by the roadside and forced to carry the heavy cross, when

Jesus was too weak to carry it. Luke reports the mournful weeping of a group of women, to whom Jesus spoke, comforting them. His words are a bit obscure as he reflects on the ordeal of suffering and turmoil of life.

The Hours Of The Cross

Arriving at Golgotha, known as the place of the skull, about the third hour of the day, i.e. 9:00 a.m., the soldiers set about their gruesome task. They offered him wine to drink, perhaps to dull the pain of crucifixion, but he refused. Stripping him naked, they nailed his body to the cross, and lifted it up. From the cross, Jesus prayed for God to forgive those who crucified him, for they did not understand what they were doing.

The morning hours emphasize the indignity of the crucifixion. A plaque identifying him as the King of the Jews was affixed to the cross, with the crowds pointing to it and laughing. The soldiers sat down at the foot of the cross to gamble for his clothing. The Jewish leaders, the bystanders who had gathered to watch the spectacle, and the pilgrims passing by mocked Jesus and taunted him. It was a macabre scene, a gruesome dance of death played out for the lurid entertainment of the unruly mob.

The irony of the crucifixion is illustrated in the account of two thieves who were crucified along with Jesus. The Roman soldiers had taken the occasion to clear out the cells of death row prisoners, executing two bandits. Luke differs from Matthew and Mark in the report. They note that both thieves joined in the mocking derision of Jesus, but Luke tells us that only one cursed him. The other rebuked his companion, admitting they deserved their fate, but Jesus was innocent. Speaking to Jesus, he asked to be remembered, and Jesus assured him of his heavenly salvation.

Darkness At Noon

At 12:00 noon the sun disappeared and an eerie, troubling darkness fell over the scene, continuing until 3:00 p.m. Matthew and Mark report that Jesus, when the pain of crucifixion was most excruciating, shouted with a loud voice, crying out in agony, "My God! My God! Why have you forsaken me?" Known as the cry of dereliction, it reflects the anguished lamentation of the penitential Psalm 22:1. It was the moment when Jesus experienced the lowest depth of agonizing pain, feeling that even God had abandoned him. He was alone in his suffering. The words with which he addressed God, "Eloi! Eloi!" were mistaken by the crowds to think he was calling the prophet, Elijah. Some offered him sour wine on a sponge; others continued their derision, asking if Elijah would come to release him. Luke reports that at this moment Jesus commended his spirit to God, and willingly surrendered his breath of life. With a loud cry, Jesus died.

Such a momentous event was marked with amazing phenomena. The veil of the temple was ripped into pieces. The curtain referred to was the hanging that separated the Holy Place from the Holy of Holies. The inner chamber was considered the most sacred place, where God dwelt. Only the high priest was ever allowed to enter, and only on the Day of Atonement. Rending the veil in two signified that Jesus had obliterated the separation of God from God's people, and made perfect access to God possible for all humankind. Matthew and Mark note that the curtain was torn from top to bottom, symbolizing that it was an act of God, who came openly to all human beings in the death of the Incarnate Son, Jesus. Matthew also reports a number of cosmic phenomena. The earth shook as with an earthquake; rocks were split into pieces. Graves were opened and the dead bodies of the saints emerged from their tombs and walked around.

The climax of the crucifixion came with a poignant confession by the centurion, who had commanded the execution squad that crucified Jesus. He declared that Jesus was God's Son. It was an ironic affirmation from an unbelieving stranger. In contrast to the Jewish leaders who sought Jesus' death because they accused him of claiming to be the Son of God, it was this pagan executioner who confessed Jesus' divine Sonship.

In counterpoint to the centurion's confession, the Gospels bring the death of Jesus to its close with the quiet notice that standing among the crowd, witnessing the crucifixion, were the women who had followed Jesus throughout his ministry from Galilee. Matthew and Mark name them as Mary Magdalene, Mary the mother of

James and Joseph, and the mother of James, or Salome. Conspicuous by their absence were the disciples, who had fled from Jesus when he was arrested.

Burial

The trail of tears ended at the tomb where Jesus was buried. Two narratives close the day of crucifixion. Joseph of Arimathea, who was a member of the council but also a follower of Jesus, asked Pilate to release the body to him, that he might bury Jesus. Discerning that Jesus was dead, Pilate granted the request. Joseph quickly prepared the body, wrapping it in a linen cloth. He laid the body in a new tomb that had been carved out of rock. Matthew tells us it was Joseph's own tomb. A large rock was rolled across the entrance to seal the cave.

It was necessary to work quickly. By Jewish custom the body had to be buried before the beginning of the Sabbath, at 6:00 p.m. There was not sufficient time to prepare the body fully by anointing it with the burial spices. The women followed the funeral procession to see where the body was entombed. Luke tells us they were planning to come later and anoint the body with the proper spices and ointments. We recall that Jesus had been anointed in anticipation of his death by the woman who poured an expensive ointment on his head at the home of Simon the leper, early in the week.

In the second narrative, recorded only by Matthew, the chief priests and Pharisees, thinking of Jesus' predictions that he would rise from the dead after three days, and suspicious of the disciples, asked Pilate for a guard to be set at the tomb. Pilate granted their request, and the guard sealed the tomb where the dead body of Jesus lay. The way of the cross was ended.

Class Members — Preparation Guide

Read the accounts of the crucifixion and make a list of what happened. Mark is the basic source. Follow Mark's unfolding drama by tracing the hours of the crucifixion.

Read Mark 15:21-39.

- Why did they give Jesus wine to drink?
- What did they do with his clothing?
- At what time was he crucified?
- What title was nailed to the cross?
- What happened at noon?
- How long did the darkness last?
- What was the cry of dereliction? Cf. Psalm 22:1.
- How did the bystanders respond to the cry of dereliction?
- At what time did Jesus die?
- What happened at the moment Jesus died?
- Who else was crucified at that time?
- How did the crowds respond to the crucifixion?
- How did the bandits crucified with him respond?

Read Luke 23:32-43.

- How does Luke's account of the thieves differ?

Cf. Matthew 27:51-53.

- What does Matthew add to the report?
- How did the centurion respond to Jesus' death?

Group Leader —
Suggestions For Class Discussion

Consider discussing the **Stations Of The Cross.**

In the city of Jerusalem, the Via Dolorosa runs from the Castle of Antonio, thought to be the location of the Praetorian, where Jesus was tried before Pontius Pilate, to the Church of the Sepulchre, traditionally considered the site of Jesus' grave, where he was buried. Since the beginning of the sixteenth century, it has symbolized the spiritual exercise known as the Stations of the Cross, initiated by the Franciscan Order.

The Stations of the Cross, as a spiritual discipline of piety and devotion, trace the path of Jesus from the house of Pilate to the gravesite via numbered way stations. Worshipers visit each station in sequence, pausing for prayer and meditation on the suffering and death of Jesus, then moving on to the next station. At each stop there may be a crude, wooden cross, a picture, or some other object of veneration, reminding the spiritual pilgrims of Jesus' road to the cross, causing them to think of each step to be recalled in meditating on the passion. Traditionally in the Roman Catholic discipline the number of stations along the way has been fourteen, although in popular piety there may be variations in both sequence and number.

In the Middle Ages, visiting the Stations of the Cross earned indulgences for the worshiper. Today the exercise is a devotional discipline for meditation and prayer. It leads us through the excruciating agony of Jesus' suffering and helps us to understand and accept the scandal of Christ crucified for us. Spiritual exercises such as this form and shape our piety, encouraging us to relive the trauma of Good Friday, and preparing us for the glorious celebration of Jesus' resurrection on Easter.

A Brief Bibliography

Barclay, William. 1975. *Introduction To The First Three Gospels.*
Philadelphia: Westminster Press.

A comprehensive reference work by an honored and respected biblical commentator known for his devotional spirit, it is a fundamental study resource helpful both to teachers and church members.

This is a new edition of Professor Barclay's earlier introduction, 1966. *The First Three Gospels.*

Binz, Stephen J. 1989. *The Passion and Resurrection Narratives of Jesus.* Collegeville, MN: The Liturgical Press.

A fine exegesis of the texts of both the Passion and Resurrection, it is a very helpful resource for Bible study and worship leaders.

Brown, Raymond E. 1986. *A Crucified Christ In Holy Week.* Essays on the Four Gospel Passion Narratives. Collegeville, MN: The Liturgical Press.

An excellent scholarly study, both academic and devotional, by one of the most respected Bible scholars of recent years, it is very helpful for church members to read.

Brown, Raymond E. 1994. *The Death Of The Messiah.* From Gethsemane to the Grave. 2 volumes. Anchor Bible Reference Library. New York: Doubleday.

An exhaustive and definitive academic study of the Passion Narratives by a recognized Roman Catholic scholar, it is a basic tool for exegesis and interpretation.

Matera, Frank J. 1986. *Passion Narratives And Gospel Theologies.* Interpreting the Synoptics Through Their Passion Stories. New York: Paulist Press.

A superb, meticulously researched and carefully written exegetical study of the Synoptic Gospels by a lesser known scholar whose thesis is that the Passion Narratives define the theology of each Gospel, it well deserves to be read by anyone seriously studying the Biblical Narratives.

Nickle, Keith F. 1980. *The Synoptic Gospels.* An Introduction. Atlanta: John Knox Press.

A fine overview of Gospel study by an author with the ability to explain technical biblical research and interpretation in terms easily understood by all.

Reddish, Mitchell G. 1997. *An Introduction To The Gospels.* Nashville, TN: Abingdon Press.

The most recent and a very readable introduction to Gospel studies, it is a fine resource for both scholars and church members.